Pebble

Countries

England

by Christine Juarez

Consulting Editor: Gail Saunders-Smith, PhD

CAPSTONE PRESS
a capstone imprint

Pebble Books are published by Capstone Press,
1710 Roe Crest Drive, North Mankato, Minnesota 56003
www.capstonepub.com

Library of Congress Cataloging-in-Publication Data
Cataloging-in-Publication information is on file with the Library of Congress.
ISBN 978-1-4765-5168-5 (paperback)

Editorial Credits
Erika L. Shores, editor; Bobbie Nuytten, designer; Tracy Cummins, media researcher;
Laura Manthe, production specialist

Photo Credits
Dreamstime: Peterguess, 22; Getty Images: Monty Rakusen, 17; iStockphotos: zoranm, 21;
Newscom: LUKE MACGREGOR, 15; Shutterstock: anshar, 1, Bikeworldtravel, 11, CBCK, 5,
Chrislofotos, 7, ekler, 4, Elena Shashkina, 13, Jonathan Feinstein, 19, Kaetana, cover, 1 (design
element), Natalia Barsukova, 22, Ohmega1982, back cover (globe), Reddogs, 9, S.Borisov, cover

Note to Parents and Teachers

The Countries set supports national social studies standards related to
people, places, and culture. This book describes and illustrates England.
The images support early readers in understanding the text. The repetition
of words and phrases helps early readers learn new words. This book
also introduces early readers to subject-specific vocabulary words, which
are defined in the Glossary section. Early readers may need assistance to
read some words and to use the Table of Contents, Glossary, Read More,
Internet Sites, and Index sections of the book.

Printed in the United States of America in North Mankato, Minnesota.
092013   007764CGS14

Table of Contents

Where Is England?

England is an island country west of Europe. England is slightly smaller than the U.S. state of Alabama. England's capital city is London.

ENGLAND

Landforms

England has rolling hills, lakes, and rivers. The Pennines are hills in central England. The rainy Lake District is to the northwest. The Thames is England's longest river.

Animals

Foxes, hares, and mice are common in England. About 230 kinds of birds make England their home. Another 200 kinds of birds pass through England as they migrate.

Language and Population

England is home to 53 million people. Cities are crowded. People live in apartment buildings or houses built in rows. Most people speak English.

11

Food

A famous English dish is shepherd's pie. It is made of ground beef and mashed potatoes. A lunch meal of fried fish and potato fries is called fish and chips.

Celebrations

November 5 is Guy Fawkes Day. Fawkes led a failed plan to destroy the Parliament building in 1605. Each year people celebrate the failure with bonfires and fireworks.

Where People Work

Most English people work service jobs as teachers, bankers, or salespeople. Tourism has many service jobs. Tourists visit museums, churches, and Buckingham Palace.

Transportation

Trains carry people to and
from train stations across England.
London has an underground
railway called the Tube.

19

19

Famous Sight

Buckingham Palace is in London. It is the official home of the ruling king or queen. The palace holds royal events and ceremonies.

Country Facts

Name: England

Capital: London

Population: 53,000,000 (2012 estimate)

Size: 50,302 square miles (130,282 square kilometers)

Language: English

Main Crops: wheat, barley, corn, rye, oats

Money: pound

England's flag

Critical Thinking Using the Common Core

1. Guy Fawkes didn't manage to do what he set out to do. Why do you think people in England celebrate the day anyway? (Integration of Knowledge and Ideas)

2. Look at the photo on page 19. Can you explain why the train system it shows might be referred to as "the Tube"? (Craft and Structure)

Glossary

capital—the city in a country where the government is based

celebrate—to do something fun on a special day

ceremony—special actions, words, or music performed to mark an important event

hare—an animal that looks like a large rabbit with long, strong back legs

island—a piece of land that is surrounded by water

landform—a natural feature of the land

language—the way people speak or talk

migrate—to move from one place to another in search of food

official—having the approval of a country or a certain group of people

Parliament—the building in London where the government is run

royal—having to do with a king or a queen

tourism—the business of taking care of visitors to a country or place

Enderlein, Cheryl L. *Christmas in England.* Christmas Around the World. North Mankato, Minn.: Capstone Press, 2013.

Rubbino, Salvatore. *A Walk in London.* Somerville, Mass.: Candlewick Press, 2011.

Simmons, Walter. *England.* Exploring Countries. Minneapolis: Bellwether Media, 2011.

Internet Sites

FactHound offers a safe, fun way to find Internet sites related to this book. All of the sites on FactHound have been researched by our staff.

Here's all you do:
Visit *www.facthound.com*
Type in this code: 9781476542287

Super-cool stuff!   Check out projects, games and lots more at
www.capstonekids.com

Index